A

CAT'S

LIFE

JUDY J. KING

A

Cat's

LIFE

Dulcy's Story

As given to
Dee Ready

Illustrated by
Judy J. King

CROWN PUBLISHERS, INC.
NEW YORK

This book is dedicated to
Mary Crum, Robert Dietrich, and Andrew Fuller.

Published by Crown Publishers, Inc., 201 East 50th Street, New York, New York 10022. Member of the Crown Publishing Group.

Manufactured in the United States of America

Designed by Nancy Kenmore

Library of Congress Cataloging-in-Publication Data

Ready, Dolores.
    A cat's life : Dulcy's story / as given to Dee Ready.—1st ed.
    1. Cats—Minnesota—Stillwater—Biography.   2. Ready, Dolores.
  I. Title.   II. Title: Dulcy's story.
  SF445.5.R43   1992
  813'.54—dc20   92-698
                                                               CIP

ISBN 0-517-58872-2

10 9 8 7 6 5 4 3 2 1

First Edition

$\mathscr{P}$ROLOGUE

At the end, all that matters is love...

*my love for my human
and hers for me.
I have planted the memories
of our life together
in her heart.
She will find them there
when I am gone and they
will comfort her.*

ℱinding Each Other

 When I was just a few weeks old, Natasha, my mother, told me that humans would come to our closet to see my sisters and brother and me. Each of us would leave the security of our box to live with one of these humans.

Soon they came. Daily they walked to the closet door, bent from their great height, and picked us up. This did not please me: They were too bold; they had no manners; they stared. We cats like to advance into relationships slowly—to look and then glance away; to look and then meditate on what was seen; to look and then rumble our approval. Or disapproval.

I could not live long years with anyone who did not know the basic rules of etiquette. Having no manners, how could any of these visitors be gracious enough to respond to my demands? I hungered for someone who would appreciate my sweet disposition and value my uniqueness.

Then, when I was seven weeks old, a female human came. She knelt and gazed with gentle eyes, yet she did not stare. Nor did she touch my brother, my sisters, or me. Giving us time to consider her presence, she placed a hand by our box so we could smell her scent.

After long moments, she settled herself on the floor and took off her shoes. Next, she ran a soothing fingertip down my back and scratched behind my ears. I discovered joy.

With slow movements that caused no alarm, she lay on her stomach, put her elbows on the floor, and rested her chin against her fists. She looked at us, then glanced away. Thus, we could assess the meaning of her gaze.

The four of us tumbled from our box and did a slow weaving dance of advance and retreat around her elbows. She lowered a hand for our inspection. Courteously she let us nip her fingers; softly she spoke to each of us. After each greeting, she awaited our answering mew. She showed, even then, that she could satisfy my needs.

Righting herself, she reached forward. I trembled. Whom would she choose? Me? Would she pick me? I wanted her for my human. Did she want me?

Yes!

Gently she cuddled me in the palm of her hand and touched the ebony patch of fur on my back with her middle finger. She riffled the white fur of my belly. She rubbed her nose against the side of my face. She curved her hand against the thrust of my black tail. She smiled at the ebb and flow of my purr.

She spoke to me in silence and touch, and I answered her with a squeaky mew of approval. At that moment I irrevocably chose her.

"You're so sweet," she said. "So sweet." Her words delighted me. After she left, I could hardly wait for her return. Daily, I dreamed my karma.

As I waited for my human to return, I listened to all my mother told me about the relationship between humans and cats. One evening, Mother curved her sleek body round us and settled into the ritual of our bath. The rumbling contentment of her purr filled my ears as she began the final stage of our education. Licking our fur, she taught us the ancient song of the cat:

I leap and laze with utter grace;
I use a paw to groom my face.
I lick my fur until it's sleek;
I try to snare the faucet's leak.
I lap my milk; I stretch and yawn;
I prowl the night from dusk to dawn.
I hiss and spit; I mew and yowl;
I greet rude laughter with a scowl.
I arch my tail to show disdain
to every cur in my domain.
I stalk my prey; I lunge; I pounce;
my daring feats to all announce.
I wear a self-sufficient air
and sharpen my claws on the
living-room chair.
I train the human with whom I live
and make my meows imperative.

This song of my birthright assured me that I would command; my human would serve. This was my destiny.

Soon she came to take me to the home where I would be imperious, and she would dedicate herself to my comfort. Thus, at the outset, did I define our life together.

$\mathscr{P}$ l a y i n g

🐾

$\mathbf{M}$y human took me to a small apartment at the top of a two-story house. In the space of the first day I had explored its rooms and discovered a sufficient number of secret places in which to hide and nap.

She was reasonably prompt in feeding me and keeping my water bowl full. She learned quickly that I was a private kitten who disliked being watched while I ate. If she stood close by as I sniffed my food, I sat back on my hind legs and stared into space until she left. If she persisted in watching me, I simply walked away from the food bowl—a tactic that took real resolve.

After eating, I dragged a string to where my human stood and dropped it in front of her. Letting the string dangle a few inches off the floor, she swung it in circles. I leaped and lunged. Then she raced through the apartment trailing the string. I galloped after her, trying to snare this elusive prey in the pincers of my teeth.

When my human dropped the string in a coil on the carpet, I tugged it beneath the chair, alert to her next move. Getting down on her hands and knees, she crawled across the floor and snatched the string. To chase, to chase! We scampered through the apartment— string, human, and me. Then we tumbled together on the floor and nuzzled.

Sometimes she pulled me across the floor on a small rug as I gripped its fringed edge in my claws. Jerking the rug to the left and then quickly to the right, she tried to dislodge me. But I held on!

Another wonderful game we played was the battle of the bag. My human took cans and small boxes from a large brown bag, then left the big bag on the floor for me to explore. Crawling into the dark interior, I trembled in anticipation. Soon she rattled the paper with her fingers. I pounced to capture the noise. She poked the bag again. I countered her foray. Finally, I collapsed into sleep.

At night we played in bed. Moving her hand to and fro beneath the sheet, my human fashioned shifty mice to mock me. I pawed their presence; I nipped their heads; I pounced on their backs; I met their challenge and prevailed.

During the long hours while I waited for my human to return from a place she called school, I explored every drawer that she left open, discovered the dark space under the bed where she never swept, investigated the plastic pitcher she used to water the plants. I crawled under the edge of the carpet and made valleys and mountains, dunes and tunnels.

When my human returned, she sometimes found a lamp askew or a throw rug tossed into a corner. She never scolded; she simply set the lamp upright and straightened the rug. Then she held me and talked about her day. Because I was still learning the human vocabulary, I could not always follow what she said about the human kits she met each day. With her voice sweetly droning in my ears, I slept.

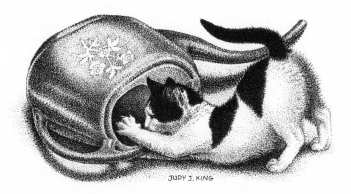

JUDY J. KING

My human did not name me. She knew that I had brought a name to life at birth and at my mother's belly. Patiently she waited for me to share this name. So on the sixth night, I laid my head close to her shoulder and spoke:

> *When Natasha first saw me,*
> *she sniffed out my name*
> *then purred me this melody,*
> *so I could proclaim—*
> *I'm Dulcinea, the sweet one,*
> *pure gift, pure delight.*
> *Dulcinea, the sweet one,*
> *with fur black and white.*
> *Dulcinea, the sweet one,*
> *a pleasure to know,*
> *Dulcinea, the sweet one,*
> *my regard I bestow*
> *on you who will welcome*
> *this name that I share,*
> *on you who will treasure*
> *the sweetness I bear.*

When I ended my song, my human picked me up with gentle hands and blew softly on my forehead. "Dulcinea—the name suits you. You are so sweet." I tapped her cheek. Truly, I had chosen well.

My human immediately shortened my name to Dulcy. This was all right because I knew that this nickname, as she called it, meant she was comfortable with me. She said we were friends. But I knew better. She was my servant; I, her mistress.

$\mathscr{D}$ i s c o v e r i n g O u r
F o i b l e s

Only one habit of my human marred our life together. She introduced me to others by saying, "This is my kitten." The statement did not please me. Clearly, she must not say "*my* kitten," "*my* cat." I was not hers. She did not *own* me. I did not *belong* to her. Quite simply, just the opposite was true: She belonged to me. She was *my* human, but I belonged only to myself. Natasha had taught me that. I had to teach her to say, "This is the cat with whom I live."

I did not think that teaching her this would be difficult for a superior cat such as myself. From the beginning she knew I was special. She told me so often. I was the smartest and sleekest kitten she had ever met.

I made her laugh. The first time I heard her laughter, I hid behind the refrigerator. But I came to understand this sign of her delight and to relish it. Often in her merriment she would say, "Dulcy, I never knew kittens could be so much fun! Why did I live alone all these years?"

The sound of my human's voice became beautiful to me, and the words of love she spoke became the highlights of my day.

Some sounds, however, like the roar of the vacuum sweeper, terrified me. Whenever I heard a strange sound for the first time, I skittered away and asked my human, "What's happening?" Picking me up, she would smooth my fur and whisper, "It's nothing to be afraid of, Dulcy. I won't let anything happen to you." I counted on that. I counted on her love.

What I did not count on was a visit to the person my human called a vet. Late one afternoon, without any warning, my human picked me up, carried me out the door, and locked it behind us.

We set off down the street. I looked forward to adventure. All around us interesting bushes and dark hiding spots beckoned. But I rested content in my human's arms. Within minutes, however, we had come to a group of buildings and were entering a place of offensive smells. The mournful sounds of desperate animals greeted us.

My human sat on a chair while I trembled in her arms. Where were we? What were these smells? Why were these animals so afraid? I smelt loneliness.

Then someone motioned for us to go into a room filled with jars. My human put me on a cold metal table. I crouched there, my legs shaking, my ears back, my fur raised. Should I attack? Even though my human's hand rested on my back, I knew fear.

A male human raised me to his face and examined my body. I hissed and spit at his smiling mask. Ignoring my swish of tail and swipe of paw, he praised my distinctive markings and my general superiority. Clearly, this human recognized a superlative kitten when he saw one. I relaxed—but only a little. Why should I trust him? What kind of human would live in this place of horrid smell and dreadful sound?

He laid me back on the bare table, and my human murmured a mystery to me. "This man is a vet, Dulcy. He won't hurt you. He just wants to give you your shots, so you won't get sick and leave me."

Never wanting to part from her, I readied myself for whatever *shots* meant. But how does one prepare for the sharp prick of the needle? For the sudden sting of the clear liquid?

Still, the distress lasted only brief seconds and my human hovered nearby. Then she lifted me in her arms, rubbed her face against my side, and announced, "It's all over, Dulcy! What a good kitten you are! You've had your first shots!"

We left the place. Mistakenly, I thought that we would never again encounter a vet. But each year afterward I endured this indignity. My only triumph is that through mighty yowls, I let my human know that this annual trip away from home did not please me.

What did please me was the fenced-in jungle of underbrush, bushes, and trees that stretched behind our apartment. On my first day in this luscious playground, I raced a few feet away from my human, skidded to a stop, and then galloped back to the safety of her delight. For long minutes she sat on the steps, encouraging me to explore.

I tumbled beneath the flower stems and leaves and made tentative forays to the end of the jungle. I hid from her and then ran, tail up, limbs stiff. My fur erect, my back legs outrunning my front so that my hind end curved forward and my body arched, I raced down the path, while my human laughed at my exuberance.

Each day I explored the secret green places and the rich black earth of this wilderness. I rolled in dust and spent lazy afternoons grooming myself. But always I returned to where my human sat on the bottom step. There I weaved my body around her feet, sniffed her fingers, and purred hello.

Bravely I met the towering challenge of trees, although the first time I climbed one, I went too high and didn't know how to get down. I howled my need, and my human, racing down the steps of our apartment, discovered my plight. She rescued me with a ladder. After that I carefully backed down trees, my pendulous tail setting the pace.

Sometimes my human would lay on her back on the jungle path and watch me climb a tree to test its highest branches. Often she would lay on her stomach while I discovered the secrets of the jungle. I found new places to hide, but always I returned to her. Her hand was gentle; her voice, soft.

$\mathscr{J}$ourneying
Together

$\mathscr{K}$

One day my human disappeared for a few hours and returned with a steel beast called a car that belched noxious fumes, roared its defiance, and leaked on the driveway. I soon learned that it moved us from place to place in a blaze of speed and a furnace of heat.

The next day, two large, noisy male humans came to remove the furniture from our apartment. Then my human packed the remaining objects into empty, but interesting, hiding places. By that evening the rooms were bare except for a sleeping bag she spread on the floor for the two of us.

Early the next morning, she carried me to the car. On the back floor she put my litter box, a bowl of water, and a container of food nuggets. Thoughtful, yes, but beyond this my human knew little about traveling with a kitten.

As we left the place my human called Dayton, Ohio, she turned on the radio. The noise it made disturbed whatever rest I had hoped for. Then she rolled down her window and the wind rushed in, moaning and howling around me. When I leaped to her lap, she quickly closed the window.

Soon the heat shimmered and I drooped on the seat next to her. She drove and drove, never stopping so I could stretch my legs or lie in the shade. Dispirited, I crawled onto her lap and mewed. She rested her hot hand on my fur but did not stop the car. Then I yowled and butted my head against her arm.

JUDY J. KING

When she recognized my weariness, she immediately stopped the car beneath a tall tree. My human opened the door, and I hurried to shade. She fetched fresh water, and I lapped its refreshment gratefully. Content, I closed my eyes. Then my human mumbled an apology. "I'm sorry, Dulcy. I should have realized you were hot. We'll drive just a little longer, then we'll stop someplace for the night."

The next day we headed north to Stillwater, Minnesota, where friends of my human lived. On this lap of our journey, she stopped often at rest places and let me investigate the terrain. After she fixed the window so that the sun did not shine in so brightly, I napped in relative comfort. I was pleased with her and with her care. And that was good because the next part of our journey tested the strength of my regard.

After spending several days with my human's friends, we drove east to New Hampshire. Throughout the morning, I moved from the softness of the front passenger seat to the shade of the backseat to the back-window ledge from where I could survey the cars trailing us. The worst part of our three-day trip was the nightmare of Lake Michigan.

Because we had left Stillwater late, we arrived at the dock as male humans herded the last cars on board the ferry. One impatiently waved us toward the loading ramp. My human gunned the motor, and we lurched and inched and careened up the ramp and into the bowels of the boat.

Someone motioned her forward to a parking space, then ordered her to get out. Heedless, she left me behind. She left me! She left *me!* Alone and defenseless in the caverns of that boat, I cowered for hours in lurking blackness while the boat shifted up and down and the cars rattled their chains. Anything could have happened to me. Anything!

I trembled at the noises and feared the worst. Wailing, I questioned my fate.

After several dismal hours, someone jumped onto the front seat, roared the engine to life, and squealed the car off the boat. I crouched behind the front seat, yowling.

Once the car stood on dry land, my human opened the door and searched for me. I squeezed myself into a tight ball and squatted beneath the seat.

"Dulcy? Dulcy?" she cried. "Where are you? You didn't jump out, did you?" Her voice trembled.

"I'm sorry, Dulcy. I'm so sorry. I forgot about you. I was so nervous when that man yelled at me that I forgot that you were loose in the car. Please don't be lost. Please be here somewhere."

Finally, she discovered me crouched beneath the front seat and tried to pull me out by my back legs. I refused to budge. With a sigh, she got into the car. As we drove away she mouthed tedious apologies about leaving me in that desperate situation.

"I'm sorry. I'm really sorry, Dulcy. I promise not to forget again. I've just never had to drive on a ferry before."

I punctuated her monologue with discordant, but effective, yowls.

After a suitable interval, I emerged from under the seat and settled beside her. She had abandoned me. True. But even as I lay imprisoned in the boat, I knew that I would never find another human who suited me so well. Were we to be separated, I should always miss her.

$\mathcal{E}$stablishing
Routines

After three days my human and I arrived in New Hampshire. We settled into a large apartment and proceeded to work out the schedule of our life together. For five straight days she was gone all day; then for two days she was home. Each night she graded the papers of her high school students.

Often we played a game. She used a pencil to do what she called writing, and I pawed the yellow cylinder, trying to capture it with my claws. She wove the pencil from left to right, taunting me. But I was adroit at seizing my prey.

After playing for a while, I fell asleep, curled next to her arm. Between naps, I stood, arched my back, and stretched to limber my body. Nonchalantly I settled down on the papers. Then she stopped her grading and talked to me.

My human's voice caressed me as she smoothed my fur and told me about her day. I learned that she did not like teaching at this New Hampshire school. "The students don't like the way I teach, Dulcy. I direct their questions back to them, and they think I'm dumb."

This puzzled me. She seemed to me—and I am trying to be as objective as possible—to be quite a fine human, someone who could laugh and sing and play. Someone who knew when to be quiet so that a cat could sleep.

I enjoyed this new apartment. My human left one window partly open so that I could leap outside and investigate the woods across the street. Time spent hunting there or napping in a patch of sunlight made the absence of my human bearable. I learned to listen for the sound of the car. Whenever I heard it, I ran from woods or bedroom or empty box to greet her.

Several times I surprised her. Once I brought a bird through the open window. When I opened my mouth, it flew to freedom. Its chirruping greeted my human when she unlocked the door.

Twice I carried a chipmunk into the apartment. Each time, the nervous creature scurried through the rooms until my human captured it in a sack and put it outside.

I did not understand why she released these animals. They were my gifts to her just as tuna was her gift to me. I ate her gifts. Why didn't she eat mine?

Still, these signs of my regard must have delighted her for when she saw them, she exclaimed, "Dulcy! What a hunter you are! The best hunter in the world!"

Thus did I share the joy of the hunt. My human came to know that often I captured and killed, while at other times I brought home to her the live trophies of the chase. Though they cowered, I did not harm these creatures that I saved for my human. I left them unscathed in the apartment, offerings for her amusement.

I hunted my human, too, in a game of hide and seek. When she returned from school, I often ran from the kitchen and scampered to a hiding place. My favorite hideouts were behind the file drawers of her desk and in the empty packing boxes stacked in the spare bedroom.

Trembling, I heard her furtive footsteps moving from room to room. As she sought my hiding place, she whispered, "Where's Dulcy? Where's that Dulcy?"

Her voice got closer and closer; I quivered with anticipation. Then she discovered me! "I see you! I see you!"

Suddenly she wheeled and ran from the room. The hunt began! Quite soon I discovered that the bathtub was her favorite place to hide. But to make the game last longer, I investigated other rooms first.

Finally, I stealthily entered the bathroom to discover her crouched in the tub, behind the partially closed shower curtain. Standing upright, I leaned my front paws on the rim of the tub and purred discovery. Then I leaped to the edge of the tub and spied her crouched body. As she raised her head, I meowed, "I found you! I found you!" Jumping to the floor, I'd run away to hide again. Ah, the joy of the chase.

$\mathcal{E}$ n d u r i n g
L o n e l i n e s s

$\mathbf{G}$rowing to adulthood, I was content. My human loved me and knew how to serve me by keeping my kitty litter clean and feeding me tuna frequently. She played with me and told me how wonderful I was. She delighted in smoothing my fur, and she found me truly exceptional. Life was good.

Good, that is, until she abandoned me again for two desolate days and two dismal nights.

When she left one morning, I assumed the day would end as usual, with her coming home to me. I did not know that anything was amiss until another human came to feed me in the late afternoon. As the hours passed and my human did not return, I panicked. Where was she? Why hadn't she come?

Except for the incident in the ferry, this was our first separation. A second day and night passed. Had she left me? Was I an orphan? Would I never see her again?

The human who came to care for me was kind. Hearing my howls, she carried me to the kitchen where she held me close and talked to me. I was too upset to thank her. Where was *my* human? Didn't she love me? Didn't she need to be with me each day and night? I needed to be with her. I now freely admitted this. I needed her.

In the early evening of the third day my human came. When the car rumbled into the driveway, I yowled my fury and delight. She was home! She had come back to me!

She raced up the stairs. Seeing me, she laughed in pure pleasure. "Dulcy! Dulcy! I missed you so. These three days seemed long!"

I leaped into her arms, nudged her chin with my head, and purred louder than I ever had before. She was home! I was not an orphan! I relished the touch of her hand on my fur; I rejoiced in the lilt of her voice.

She carried me to our bed and lay down. I crawled over and around her; from her feet to her head I explored and sniffed and licked. Prodding her face with mine, I pushed against her chin, turned circles on her stomach, and kneaded her T-shirt. My human was home!

Smoothing my fur, she scratched beneath my chin and crooned a song. She told me about her journey away from me. She said my name over and over: "What's your name? What's your name? Are you Dulcy? Are you the sweet one?"

Minutes passed and still I claimed her full attention. Finally, I plotted another map on her stomach and collapsed to sleep—my first contented sleep since she had disappeared three days before. She slept, too. When we awoke, she fed me. Then she crawled beneath the blanket, and I curved myself around her head. As we slept through the night, I forgot my fear.

Still, my need puzzled me. I had not counted on loving her so. But I would maintain my rule. She must not leave me orphaned. I would settle this once and for all; I would teach her who was mistress, who slave. I would teach her the six commands that would help her serve me in our life together.

Training
Together

✿

Thus far, our life together had been so enjoyable that I had forgotten the advice Natasha gave me: Make your meows imperative. I had been negligent with my human, not following through on my commands, not insisting that she listen and learn. Now began a period of concentrated instruction.

Because she was human, I knew she could not learn to speak cat, a language far too subtle for her. I did not have years to teach her its nuances. If I were to lead a comfortable life, with all my needs and desires attended to, I had to groom her quickly but simply. She had to listen carefully to the tenor of my meows, mews, wails, chirrups, purrs, howls, and yowls. She had to learn the modulation of my body language, the thrust of my whiskers, the frown of my forehead. She had to follow the instruction of my tail—my black baton.

I began with six elementary commands. These signals were a secret between my human and me so I cannot reveal the accompanying sound or the position of my baton. Suffice it to say that for each command I used a different sound and held my tail in a slightly different way. Nuance is everything.

Despite the ever-open window, I sometimes chose to go outside through the door. Therefore, I began my human's training with an immutable command. I stepped to the door, sat on my hind legs, and meowed "Let me out." After I did this with great deliberation for several days, she heard the difference between this and the other meows I was teaching her. She responded in an entirely suitable fashion by rushing to the door and opening it.

As time passed, I did not even need to go near the door. If she were reading—which she did a lot—I simply stood before her and meowed this command. She quickly put down her book, carried me to the door, sat me before it, and opened it. However, I would not immediately cross the threshold.

No. First, I peered around the edge of the door and sniffed for signs of that yapping, barking brute called a dog—a creature with teeth twelve inches long and no manners. Had he invaded my domain? Only after a thorough investigation would I decide either to go out or stay in. The true test of a well-trained human is whether she will patiently wait while a cat sniffs. My human did.

The second strategic command was "Let me in." I made this yowl especially pathetic, as if I were in considerable pain. Hearing the cry, my human rushed to the door. The first time she came, she opened it too fast and swatted me. Twit!

My angry cry brought an appropriate response. She scooped me up, babbled an apology, and vowed to be more careful in the future. Thus I trained her to open the door only a crack so that I might slip through like a wraith. I paused just inside the door so that she could carry me to my food bowl.

My third command had to do with food. With twitch of tail, frown of forehead, and rumble of voice, I demanded "Feed me. Now." This command brought excellent results. Seldom did my human feed me anything unsavory.

Because of my adventuresome nature, I liked many watering holes. Therefore, I taught my human a fourth command—to place water wherever I wanted it. When I determined a new location, I went to this site and sat with a regal tilt to my head and an expectant coil of my tail. Then I meowed softly, stopping after each brief mew to look at her. Soon she ran for water.

The fifth command—"Smooth my fur"—was essential to my well-being and to be done only on my terms. During training, I frequently jumped onto my human's lap, turned a few circles, kneaded her thighs, and then settled to nap. Always she responded by stroking me. Uncalled for! Immediately, I jumped to the floor and stalked away.

After waiting a few minutes, I returned to her lap. This time I purred, nudged her hand, and curled my tail around my body. When she stroked my fur, I stayed. Ah, the difference. She learned never to place her hands on my fur unless I gave these three clear signals.

Because of this command I was able to sleep without her hand resting on me. Whenever she forgot and placed the weight of her fingers on my fur, I immediately cleaned myself or jumped down from her lap. Yes, a hard command to teach. But necessary.

My human's response to the sixth and final command pleased me. Sometimes I craved the feel of her fingernails beneath my chin. I employed facial and tail gestures and a lengthened meow to teach this command. After meowing, I rubbed my chin against her hand and swished my tail slowly back and forth. Quickly she learned to scratch under my chin while I stretched my head backward and purred with delight.

Thus passed our period of training. I was patient; she was, I may say, highly educable.

Instructing my human in these six voiced commands was not enough, however. She had to learn my silence.

Instead of meowing "Let me out," I sat by the door, still as a statue. Slowly my silence shattered her preoccupation and she rushed to respond to my needs.

Another silent command my human learned quite well was "Open this drawer for me to explore." I taught her this by dint of sitting patiently and quietly before a dresser. I'd gaze at the drawer intently for a while, then turn my head and stare at her. Ultimately the depth of my stillness captured her attention. A cat's silence is powerful!

In all this training, I held to one underlying belief: I was in command of our relationship. When my human called my name, I ignored her. From where I lay, I heard her cry, "Dulcy! Come in now! Please." With a slight, somewhat disdainful twitch of an ear, I let her know that the sound of her entreaty had reached me.

Still, I did not turn toward her. After a suitable amount of time, however, I licked my fur, stood and stretched, lazily swayed my tail to right and left, and nonchalantly sauntered to where she stood. Thus did I rule.

$\mathcal{E}$ n c o u n t e r i n g
P a i n

◦

$\mathbf{O}$ne fall day something happened that changed me forever. In the morning I explored the landlord's car, which sat in the driveway. I crawled into its dark and smelly belly where I settled and slept. Suddenly the car bellowed. Pain stabbed. I fell to the driveway. With my throbbing tail hanging by a thin thread of skin and fur, I lurched to the comfort of my human's bed. Blood spotted the quilt. All day I lay in misery, longing for her voice and touch.

Hours later she came. When I heard her key in the door, I staggered into the kitchen.

"Dulcy! Did you have a good day?"

I moaned. Quickly she picked me up and discovered my drooping tail, almost lost to me.

"What happened, Dulcy?" she cried. "You must be in terrible pain! We've got to do something!"

We rushed outside. I struggled against the confines of her arms. Never again did I want to ride in a car. Never again would I trust such a malevolent beast.

As my human drove, she eased my fears by holding me against her shoulder and murmuring, "It's all right, Dulcy. You're going to be all right. I'll protect you. It's all right. No one's going to hurt you."

When my human carried me in to meet the vet, I took an instant dislike to him. He was too hearty. He told my human to hold me on the table while he prepared a syringe. She held me gently. But he did not give the shot as the vet in Dayton had. He did not stretch my skin taut. He simply towered over me, lunged downward, and plunged the needle into my quivering body.

Frightened by the sudden shock of pain, I jumped straight up, then crashed to the floor. Lurching from wall to cabinet to corner, I dragged my almost-severed tail behind me. The offending needle wobbled in my back. Finally I collapsed as my human shouted, "What do you think you're doing? That's not the way to give a shot! You idiot! Dulcy's in pain. What's wrong with you?"

When I woke, I lay in a smelly box with metal bars. I smelled too. As I groomed my fur, I realized that my tail was gone.

The hours of the night passed and morning came. Would I spend forever in this cage with these pitiful nuggets of unappetizing food and the odors of ether and canine? Would I ever see my human again?

Finally she came and removed me from that place of pain and horrible smells and sounds. I was weary and could not lick her hands. Even my purr was tired. But she held me and sang me a song of her love:

> *Dulcy,*
> *I love you.*
> *Dulcy,*
> *I'm sorry your tail is gone.*
> *Dulcy,*
> *you are still the most*
> *beautiful cat in the world!*

Celebrating Christmas Apart

In early winter we moved again. Quite frankly, I was weary of migrating. But my human demanded that we live with two strangers. "You'll like this new place, Dulcy," she promised. "It's a farm. You can prowl the fields, and the barn has lots of mice. I'll save money living with these teachers and have some company. Besides yours, I mean. It's going to be an adventure, Dulcy."

Clearly, she did not understand that cats want to stay in a place that is familiar and known; its secret places found and investigated; its odors discovered and identified.

Despite my initial doubts, the farm turned out to be a challenging place to live, full of hiding places and dark shadows, warm sunlight and tantalizing smells, long vistas and tasty mice (as my human had promised).

Much happened to me on the farm. I grew from kit to cat; I experienced my first winter; and I learned how unpredictable my human was.

In midwinter, she packed her suitcase again. I tried to forestall the inevitable by lying in it, but she only laughed and deposited me on the bed. I immediately leaped back inside its walls, but she persisted in filling it with jeans and T-shirts. Finally, despite all my diversionary tactics, she closed the case and set it by the door. She was leaving again.

JUDY J. KING

The next day, however, she placed both me and the suitcase in the car. Ah! Perhaps we were going on another journey together. Although I didn't relish moving, I wanted to be with her wherever she went.

But that wasn't to be. After a while she stopped the car, and I caught the pungent odor of other animals. She picked me up, walked into a squat building, and said, "It's Christmas, Dulcy, and I'm going to visit our friends in Stillwater. I'll be gone for two weeks. But I'll be back. I promise."

She kissed the top of my head, smoothed my fur, and tried to look into my eyes. But I looked away. What did I know of two weeks? What assured her return?

The dreary days passed. She did not come. Why had she left me here among all these neglected cats and barking canines, among these overpowering smells, in this small cage where I could not roam the night? When would two weeks be up?

More days passed and I stopped eating. I lay listless in the cage and slept. I did not raise my head to sniff the beefy shreds of food that the female human put in my cage. I did not groom myself. I spent days in a dream world of longing.

A human lifted my unkempt body from the cage and rocked me. She begged me to eat. She brushed my fur. But she was not *my* human. She did not bring me the comfort of the familiar, the security of home. My face grew gaunt and my body thin; I lived in misery. I faced a life without my human. In the bleak hours of night I moaned the question that tormented me:

> *Shall I abandon you?*
> *You who have left me alone*
> *in this stark place of bitter smell*
> *and narrow cage?*
> *No. Never.*
> *Still, the question haunts me,*
> *taunts me —*
> *Have you abandoned me?*

I could not believe she would do this. No, not my human. I must live to see her return to me, to welcome her back. And so I faced the day and tried to find within myself some desire for food. But even though I had resolved to live, I had no appetite.

And then, late one afternoon, she came. Brought from the cage to the room where she stood, I yowled my welcome. She was back! She'd come back for me! She had not abandoned me.

"Dulcy!" she said. "Dulcy, I've missed you so much." She cuddled me against her chest. Then she held me away and looked deep into my eyes. "But you've lost weight, Dulcy. What happened?"

Trembling with love, I flung myself against her chest and clawed my way to her shoulder. My human had returned! I was not an orphan.

Laughing, she carried me to the car. "Dulcy! It's so good to see you. I love you more than I ever thought possible." She pressed my whiskers back against my face; she scratched beneath my chin and kissed my forehead.

"Dulcy! Dulcy! The woman told me that you didn't eat. You could have died!" I heard the fear in her voice. She knew now the depth of my love. And so did I.

As we drove away from that place of exile, I stood on my human's lap, my front paws against her chest. Again and again, I butted her face with my nose.

My human was home. Being apart from her for those two weeks had been the hardest experience of my life—harder than hunkering down in the belly of the ship, harder than losing my tail, harder than moving so many times. In those long hours of separation, I came again to know my need.

In the few months of my life I had come to love my human intensely. I wanted her close each day. I wanted to end the night by patting her face; I wanted to begin my nightly adventures from her bed. I wanted her voice to bless my exploring and to soothe my sleeping. All this I learned when she went away and left me alone and bereft.

Discovering
Loss

As winter lengthened into spring, I experienced a strange longing. Others must have noticed it, too, because many male cats sauntered into the barn and invited me to play. Whenever my human was home, I introduced the day's visitor to her.

Always I enacted the same ritual: I walked regally toward her. Behind me, and at an appropriate distance, the male of the day followed. I stopped at her feet and turned my head to look back at him. Then I meowed his name to her. She bent and scratched the fur around my ears. Then she spoke to the supplicant: "How are you?"

She always waited politely for his answer and then continued the conversation. "I'm glad to see that you recognize a superior cat when you meet one! Dulcy makes me happy, too!"

After a suitable interval in which my human praised both of us—the male cat for being discerning enough to recognize my worth and me for being so courteous and clever—I turned around and led my admirer back to the barn. The male my human particularly liked was the one I finally picked to be the father of my kits.

After I began to carry the kits within me, the male cats stopped coming. I did not miss them; I was content to be with my human as spring came. It was almost my birth day.

Drowsy with the mystery growing within me, I slept often in a patch of sun beneath a window in the living room. Waking to groom my fur, I purred the song that came instinctively to me as the kits snuggled in my womb:

> *Kits will I mother—*
> *lick their soft fur,*
> *summon their*
> *birthnames*
> *refine their sweet purr.*

> *Kits will I mother—*
> *teach them to pounce,*
> *tell them the story*
> *of curs we denounce.*

> *Kits will I mother—*
> *show them the prowl,*
> *sing them the secrets*
> *of hiss, spit, and yowl.*

Almost two months passed while the kits grew inside me. Then one day, as I mounted the basement steps, the muscles of my body pushed a wet kit onto the landing. Quickly I found my human and meowed piteously to tell her something was wrong. She had understood this meow when my tail was almost cut off; perhaps she would again.

Frightened, I led her to the basement door where the tiny kit that had once nestled in my body lay. Born too soon, it was dead. My human wrapped it in a paper towel and gathered me in her arms. We went to the vet.

This was not the vet who had stabbed me with a needle and stolen my tail. Still, I trembled as he laid me on a cold metal table and examined me. I implored my human, "Don't let him hurt me."

She whispered my name. "He won't hurt you, Dulcy. I won't let him."

He touched my stomach with probing fingers. "What's happening?" I asked her.

The vet let her hold me for a moment. "I love you, Dulcy," she said. "Don't worry—everything will be all right. Don't be afraid. No one will hurt you." Then he told her that I was going to lose all the kits. All!

She left me. Again I knew the loneliness of the steel cage and the loss of freedom. I did not like the pungent odors of ammonia and excrement and the barking of dogs. I did not like having strangers handle me. I did not like being away from my human.

That night all my kits were born dead. I lost them all. The vet gave me a shot that made me sleep, and while I slept, he did something that left black thread punctuating my stomach. Another day and night passed. The next evening my human came. Dispirited, we returned to the farmhouse. Never again would I carry kits within me.

Now I found a new song to purr, a dirge filled with the melancholy of loss:

> *Gone,*
> *gone all my kits, my little ones,*
> *before the birthing day.*
>
> *Empty,*
> *empty am I of kits and dreams;*
> *my ancient songs are stilled.*

Meeting the Great God of Cats

Days passed and in the promise of spring the visit to the vet faded; desolation paled. Still I could sing no songs; dream no dreams. The kits were gone. Then one evening a wonderful thing happened to me and my human.

When my human came home from school each day, she ate supper. Then she and I went for a walk—either in the fields or down the dirt road. Late one evening, when dark had settled around us, she and I ambled down the rutted road toward a stand of birch trees that some humans had been cutting down.

Because my human could not see well in the dark, I walked a few feet ahead so that she could follow the gleam of my white fur in the moonlight. Still, I frequently strolled to the edge of the road to sniff the wildflowers, the grass, the weeds, the rocks.

At length, we came to an opening in the wooden fence that bordered the road. Beyond the railing, a large tree lay on its side. Moonlight cast fingers of shadows. Together we walked to the fallen trunk. My human sat on it while I investigated the growth beneath it.

Soon, however, I meowed "Hold me."

My human picked me up and held her face against mine. We gazed at the moon and at the stand of birches in which we sat. Silence made us one. Quietly I purred my contentment.

Then a wondrous thing happened. Suddenly a mighty wind blew through the night forest. Trees shuddered at its embrace; leaves trembled in awe; grass bowed in the presence of glory. With a roar, the god of cats spoke to us. The whirr of her purr filled my ears; the whoosh of her tail ruffled my fur. Her majesty swept over my human and me in a whirlwind of encompassing sound.

Within moments, silence camped about us. The roar of the god of cats faded into night. Bemused, I settled on my human's lap and we rested in perfect communion. I allowed my eyes to close. My human and I had heard the god of cats. We belonged together and together we would soon know something new and great. What else could this visitation by the god of cats mean?

The gift of the god was Bartleby. He appeared the next day. Perhaps the great god thought that my human was not sufficient company for an uncommon cat such as myself.

Whatever the reason, I remained gracious to Bartleby all his life and even came to like him. And in the condition in which he came to the farm that wasn't easy! Dirt matted his fur; mites webbed his ears; mucus smeared his nose; fluid glazed his eyes. He was young—about five weeks old—and undernourished, so thin that his eyes bugged. But despite his pathetic condition, I wanted the great god of cats to whisk him away in another mighty roar of wind.

That didn't happen.

My human brought this pitiful kit into the house and let me sniff him. He smelled foul. Then she carried both of us to the couch where we sat for endless minutes. She tried to explain why she had introduced this interloper into my life, but her words rang false.

"Someone left him in a bag in the woods, Dulcy, and a woman found him. He would have died there. We can give him a home, and you can teach him all you know. Believe me, you're going to like him. It's going to be fun living with two of you!"

Fun? It was going to ruin my life!

Soon my human carried Bartleby to the bathroom. I followed. After his bath, she wiped him dry. This brought surprise. Beneath the dirt lay beauty.

When my human put Bartleby on the floor, I licked his fur. He purred and rubbed against me. Just for a moment a distant memory of a box in a closet and the warmth of Natasha came back to me. Just for a moment the ancient dream made me tender.

In that moment, I adopted him.

For a rival, Bartleby was, I may say, both gentle and unassuming. He wanted only to give pleasure—to make both my human and me happy. I felt warmhearted toward him for he knew his place—subservient to me. His exquisite manners kept him from coming to the kitty litter when I was there or from eating the food in my bowl.

I felt no anger toward Bartleby. After all, the great god of cats had sent him as a gift to me. I was a year older than he and much bigger. I could demonstrate how to train a human, how to hunt and kill, how to leap with perfect grace.

Now, as Bartleby looked to me for guidance, the songs, the dreams, came back. With his warm body pressed to my side, I sang him the ancient song of the cat. He became the kit lost to me; he became my own.

In the New Hampshire farmhouse, we lay together on the floor in a warm patch of sunlight from the east window. When he was old enough to leave the house, I introduced him to the barn and my favorite mouse hole. I encouraged him to use the litter in the basement and not the ashes in the fireplace—he seemed to like the latter better. I taught him how to groom himself so that his long fur lay rich and soft against his agile body.

From my year-old vantage point, I taught Bartleby to deal with the vagaries of vets, the sneakiness of mice, the churlishness of canines.

As Bartleby grew from kit to cat, I tried to teach him the six commands that my human knew, but he seemed reluctant to use them, and I had no tail with which to train him to the nuances of cat language. However, he was adept at expressing his wishes with eyes, whiskers, and forehead. Moreover, he never learned the art of

silence: He needed always to talk to my human and to tell her of his day. He followed her around the house when she cleaned, paced with her when she talked on the telephone, sat on her lap when she ate.

I delighted in his antics. He was a gift from the god. But still, my human could not see: He was child; I was friend.

So, as the days and months passed, Bartleby endeared himself to me. Unfortunately, he also endeared himself to my human.

When she held him, he licked her fingers and face. (My tongue never served as her washcloth!) When she came home from her school, she picked him up and smoothed his fur and called him a joy. When she graded papers, she let him curl around her tea cup. When we walked, she carried him on her shoulder.

Let her shoulder Bartleby. I would pad ahead and never scurry back to her.

Let her turn to Bartleby. I would turn away whenever she came into a room; I would refuse to purr when she scratched under my chin.

Let her talk to Bartleby. I had better things to do—like laying siege to a new mouse hole in the barn.

Let her lie with Bartleby on her chest. I would sleep on the blue down vest. It was soft. (That it carried her smell of aloe and yellow soap and baby powder was beside the point.)

Let her sleep with Bartleby on her pillow. I would lie on the couch downstairs and plot revenge.

I needed no one. I would become aloof. I would practice disdain. Surely, surely, she would respond.

I spent the days roaming the fields around the farmhouse and hunting the elusive mouse. I brought home no surprises for my human. Instead, I devoured whatever I caught. But as I prowled and pounced and pinioned, I turned my loneliness for her into a defiant yowl:

Never enough!
I was never enough for her.
She dared to bring another
between us.
Bartleby, the gentle one.
Bartleby, gift from the god.
How could I reject him?
I cannot.
But she,
she will I shun,
the human who does not know
the godsend of my love.

Coexisting

In my second summer, my human, Bartleby, and I returned to Stillwater. By now she had learned how to travel with cats. She stopped often to let Bartleby and me stretch our legs. I always headed toward the back of the rest areas. Leading the way, I wandered through deep grass and dense bushes mysterious with shadows.

My human followed behind with Bartleby (he never became much of an explorer). She either carried him or watched closely as he walked beside her. I wandered through high grass and shadow-filled bushes. Soon my human grew alarmed. "Dulcy, come back. I'm afraid you'll get lost. Come back to me."

I ignored her pleas. Still, I slowed my stealthy expedition into the underbrush—a tactic that gave her time to crash through the brambles and pick me up. She carried me to the car. I rewarded her with silence. I was fashioning aloofness into an art.

"Dulcy, why don't you talk to me?" she'd ask. Talk to her! Why didn't *she* give me the love I craved? Why didn't she give me the place in her life that would fill my loneliness? Why? She, too, then began to feel the stab of rejection.

We settled in a small apartment on the North Hill. Here I learned a new word—free-lance. My human stayed home each day, and I lay on the windowsill and watched her work. Sometimes she tried to talk to me. But I always moved to another sunny place when she approached. Despite her treachery, however, I liked having her home each day. Still, I ignored her.

Early that winter my human went away again. As she packed her suitcase, she said, "I'm going home to Independence for Christmas, Dulcy. Remember last year? I know it's a long time, but I've got to go. My father is sick. But remember, I came back last year. And I'll come back again. I'll always come back."

But that promise did not still my craving for her presence.

Someone came each day to feed Bartleby and me. I paid no attention to this person. This was not my human. Despite my misery, however, I ate and did not starve myself as I had done in that kennel in New Hampshire when she had deserted me.

Bartleby and I shared each dismal day and spoke of the perfidy of humans. My experience, of course, had not been his. Still, he listened. (Bartleby was always a good listener.) Loneliness came, but not the desolation of that long separation and confinement in New Hampshire.

Nevertheless, I turned my back and refused to greet her when she returned. Stalking to the door, I stood in awful silence until she opened it. Then I disappeared into the snowy landscape for three whole days. Always before I had returned each morning to my human, but this time I left her to distress.

I found a bush that provided shelter from the wind. I slept, caught a foolish mouse who ventured out into the windy night, and settled again into the leeward side of the house by the shrubbery. The wintry landscape lured me from this human who did not recognize my love, but her pull was stronger. She was home and world to me.

So on the morning of the fourth day, I stepped to the door and yowled. My human hurtled down the steps. She was, you may say, happy to see me. Still, she did not devote herself wholly to me on that day—the day I proved that I would never abandon her.

I knew only sadness.

As spring arrived, and then summer, I spent much of the time outside, away from my human. One autumn day a tiger cat sank its sharp teeth into my back. Soon the wound throbbed and ached.

I kept this pain to myself. I did not approach my human for comfort or love. I did not ask her to stroke behind my ears. And so she left me to my solitude.

One morning I lay on the windowsill, longing for the touch of her hand. Why exile myself? Why lie in misery? With love glazing my eyes, I reached out to her in silence so loud she could hear. Glancing toward me, she came immediately.

She rubbed her palm over my fur. Her gentle fingers found the abscess that festered on my lower back. At her touch I felt love so strong my heart melted within me. Truly, whether she knew it or not, she was *my* human.

"Dulcy, you've been in a fight! This lump is big. It must really hurt."

Once again we visited a vet. He put me to sleep, and when I awoke, my wound did not throb so much. Soon my human came for me. They talked for a while. Though I was drowsy I heard him say something about cats and infection and dying. I could smell her fear.

Confronting the Cur

During my third winter, I gained weight. My human kept my bowl full of tasty morsels. And my dejection sent me to the pantry often. When spring came, I could no longer jump to the windowsill with ease.

That fourth spring of my life, a pack of canine brutes discovered me beneath a bush one night. I howled for my human, but she slept on.

I know she would have come if she had heard me.

The dogs yapped and sniffed my scent. They pawed my lair. Their baying frightened me. Their cruel teeth gleamed; their bodies writhed in anticipation. And so I bolted to a nearby tree. The pack raced after me. Had my tail trailed behind me, they would have seized it in their savage jaws and shaken me into eternity.

JUDY J. KING

Five feet from the tree I leaped onto its bark. Even my weight did not keep me from scampering upward to the safety of a high branch. Below, the dogs growled their vexation. All night they waited at the foot of the tree, their dark shapes menacing. But even in my fear, I hissed defiance:

> *Away!*
> *Go away,*
> *you cur,*
> *you brute,*
> *you beast.*
> *I will not be*
> *a feast*
> *for your sharp fangs.*
> *Away,*
> *away with you.*
> *Leave me in peace.*

As the night wore on the shadows of dogs melted away.

In the morning I heard my human calling, "Dulcy! Dulcy! Where are you?"

I howled. Within seconds she stood below me, peering up into the branches where I crouched. "Dulcy, come down. Come on down now."

But I couldn't. Fear riveted me to the tree. Somewhere the curs lurked, eager to pounce.

All day I waited for my human to climb the tree and rescue me. I could not climb down to her. My claws would not let go of the trunk.

I spent another night in the tree and then another. Day and night my human beseeched me to come down. I could not move.

The next afternoon, some humans wearing red hats stepped from the largest truck I had ever seen. They set a ladder against the tree. One climbed up and took me into his arms. Frantically I peered over his shoulder. Where were the dogs?

My human awaited me. "Dulcy! Are you all right? It's okay. No one's going to hurt you." I trembled. Where were they?

She took me home. Weary, I slept all night and the next day. But often I felt her tender hand on my fur.

During that spring, Bartleby, my human, and I began again, after the long winter, to spend each evening walking on the North Hill. This was a habit from our first autumn there. Every agreeable day, we roamed the neighborhood together. My human stayed on the sidewalk while Bartleby and I reconnoitered the yards. Other humans watched us from their porches and greeted us. I wandered through each yard, exploring the bushes, trailing bugs, smelling the furtive enemy. Always I raced to the safety of my human when I sniffed the canine or heard its growl. Knowing my fear, my human picked me up and held me safe. At those times I settled gratefully in her arms and forgot, just for a moment, that I chose to be aloof.

Responding to My Human's Pain

That spring—my fourth—we left the North Hill. How wearisome to desert its hiding places and its familiar smells. My human explained that we would have more room in this new apartment on the south side of town.

"It's upstairs again, Dulcy, so you can survey the whole neighborhood. There are more windows to sleep in and more patches of sunlight!"

The place was big. The rooms provided an enormous space for Bartleby and me to explore together. He had grown into an interesting cat, and I found him quite satisfactory company as I ignored my human. While he did not fulfill my need, his presence brought some comfort.

But life began to change. As the days passed in this new apartment, I chose to abandon aloofness. I had to, for my human needed me. Now she often cried at night. Sometimes her sadness seemed so deep that I went to her and jumped on her lap so she could hold me.

Standing upright, I rested my front paws against her chest. Then I purred my love as I nudged her face and gently licked her cheek. She spoke with faltering words.

"Dulcy, it's just that I'm so sad. I wish I liked myself more. I wish there were more to like."

This was strange to me for I found her quite satisfactory in everything but her willingness to love only me. Still, we had years to be together. If only she were happier now. If only she were the human I had known when I was a kit.

To comfort her, I slept again in the crook behind her knees. In every way I knew, I let her know that her sorrow saddened me. I gave her all the love I'd withheld.

When she held me, I looked into her eyes and purred "Don't worry so; I love you." These were the words she needed to hear. But she still did not know cat. She could not hear the nuance of meow; she could not decipher the sway of the stub that was my tail.

Bleak days turned into months. Her spirit faded. My human's father had died and she mourned him. But something more caused this darkness.

Now no singing filled our house—and she loved to sing. No laughter rang through the rooms—and she had always laughed. No company came to visit—and she had always invited people for supper. My human walked alone.

That fall, she went away for several weeks. One monotonous day followed another. She had promised to return. But unexpected things happened to humans. Had she forgotten? Would she come home to me? Now that I'd let myself love again, my need for her grew intense.

From deep within my heart came a new song of loneliness. I keened my desolation:

Where are you, my human?
I miss you so.
Come home now, my human.
I'm here, you know.
Here at home grieving

so lonely, morose,
mournful, unhappy,
needing you close.
Come home now, my human.
Dulcy is here.
Come home now, my dear one,
Be ever near.

Finally, she returned. Seeing her smile, I leaped into her arms. Nestling against her warmth, I thrust my nose against her cheek, pawed her sweater, rejoiced in the security of her arms.

She lay down on the bed and gathered me to her chest. I licked every spot of skin I could find. Rubbing her nose against mine, she laughed. Holding me into the air, she chortled, "Are you Dulcy? Are you the sweet one?"

My human had come home. And she was happy again. So was I. No longer would I be aloof; no longer would I deny myself the joy of her presence; no longer would I pursue loneliness. She needed me just as I needed her. That was enough. Even with Bartleby, that was enough.

Meeting
Catastrophe

Soon after, we moved again — to the South Hill of Stillwater. I immediately felt at home in this large house with its two stories. My human put the kitty litter in the basement, which had an inviting crawl space underneath the kitchen.

My human knew that cats need to roam. I believe she chose this house and its neighborhood to give me sufficient room for prowling. From the beginning, she left one of the basement windows open at night. Each evening, I leaped through the opening and found the hiding places in the yard where delicious morsels of mouse and chipmunk and mole lived. How fearful they became of one with such sharp teeth and keen ears.

That summer, the human family who lived in Independence visited — two adults and four noisy kits invaded our house, played loud music, danced around the furniture, and ran through the yard without looking where they were going. A cat wasn't safe with them around.

Their presence shocked Bartleby. While my human liked to sing, she was never raucous. Our house had always been quiet and peaceful. The rowdiness of these human kits proved too much for my friend. He slunk to the basement and disappeared into the crawl space.

Three days later he demonstrated his chagrin. What an exhibition! Bartleby—gentle, happy, joyous Bartleby—emerged from hiding, purposefully mounted the basement stairs, padded into the living room, and strode to its center. When his silence drew everyone's attention, he proved his pique—by vomiting on the carpet!

Scampering away from the astounded humans, Bartleby rushed down the basement steps and jumped into the crawl space. I still enjoy his assertiveness. How proud I was of him!

My human now spent time away from Bartleby and me each day. When she first began going to work, she explained, "I'm not freelancing anymore, Dulcy. I'll be gone during the day. But I'll come home at night." She left us daily, but always returned, eager to see us, happy to be home.

The days passed. I had accepted my place in my human's life and had come to cherish Bartleby. He and I knew one another's ways. We grew older together; soon Bartleby was six and a half and I was the elder by a year. Settled into our lives, we needed no one but my human.

And then one autumn afternoon she bounded into the house. Picking me up, she babbled, "I've a surprise! We're going to have a kitten!"

What?

Then she brought in Tybalt. Like me, he was black and white. However, there our resemblance ended. I had never disgraced myself by being mean to others or malicious, conceited, and sneaky.

He took over the house.

When my human sat in her rocker, he shoved Bartleby aside and leaped onto her thighs. He cruelly sharpened his claws on her jeans and settled complacently on her lap. With a smug look, he swiped his paw at Bartleby, who sat on the floor looking longingly at my human.

Always she had given Bartleby special love. Now Tybalt took her time, hoarded her attention. Bartleby was bemused by this turn of events. I was chagrined.

Daily I watched Tybalt demonstrate his bad manners. He jumped on the kitchen table and attacked my human's food as she ate. To keep Tybalt away from her plate, she hovered over it. As she took each bite, she swept her arm across the table to push Tybalt back. Even after this, she praised his liveliness.

Praised him! The interloper!

She even brought home a scratching pole — a tall one with places to rest and hide. For him, she did this! For this troublesome, vexatious, irritating, plaguey, disagreeable, noxious, bothersome cat! How could she be so dense and dull?

She had committed the ultimate offense. I knew that I was not enough for her. I had assumed, however, that Bartleby and I together completed her. That she needed yet another cat astounded me, angered me, and yes, grieved me. Would she never be content?

*C*hoosing
Loneliness Again

Days passed and Tybalt slowly re-
vealed himself as hateful and selfish and pushy. While eating a
sandwich one day, my human rested her hand on the arm of the
rocker. In his attempt to gorge himself, Tybalt leaped up and bit
right through her finger!

Bartleby and I devised two very different methods to deal with
this intruder. Bartleby decided to act like Tybalt. Not that Bartleby,
loving cat that he was, could ever become such a despotic boor. But
Bartleby did begin jumping on the table at mealtime to claim my
human's attention.

When he did this, my human scolded Bartleby. She laughed
at Tybalt yet she reproached Bartleby and told him he should
know better! Who can understand the ways of humans? If I can't, no
one can.

Tybalt had a wild and piercing meow—once heard, never forgotten. He shrieked and screeched and squealed and screamed, always
in a rage to have his needs met. My human eagerly responded to his
demands. And so, to make my human notice him once again,
Bartleby began to meow loudly too.

As the days passed and Tybalt grew more offensive, Bartleby
became increasingly ingratiating in his attempts to please my hu-

man. In fact, he let her develop a parlor trick that would embarrass any but the most phlegmatic of felines.

For any and all visitors, my human threw Bartleby up in the air as if he were an inanimate ball. His fur puffed out around him, and he spread his legs wide before falling downward. Catching him before he hit the floor, my human crowed with glee.

Unhappy because of her neglect, Bartleby participated fully in this mortifying demonstration of how a human can make a cat look foolish.

My plan for dealing with Tybalt was simpler and more dignified. Still, it took great effort on my part because in the past year I had abandoned my policy of aloofness and once again freely gave love to my human.

Now, to rid myself of this poacher, I disappeared into the pantry, where my human fed us. It was outfitted with two long shelves, a washer, and a dryer. During the winter months that followed Tybalt's arrival, I spent my days and nights on the top shelf. When my human did the laundry, I stared at her until she began to plead, "Dulcy, try to like him. He's just a kitten. Come on. Come down."

I ignored her.

But from the confines of my prison, I wailed a malediction throughout the day. I knew that my human would not understand the words, but I was sure she would recognize the sentiments:

> *Scoundrel,*
> *Ruffian,*
> *Boor, Brute, and Beast!*
> *May the yowl of the cat*
> *desert you;*
> *the teeth of the cur*
> *devour you;*
> *the itch of the mange*
> *decay you.*
> *May you know only noise*
> *and sleepless nights.*
> *May you dirty your fur*
> *and lose all your fights.*
> *May my human forget you*
> *and give you no food.*
> *May you fall forever*
> *into servitude.*

When Tybalt entered the pantry, I damned him with yowls. Before he was grown, he cringed at my curse. Later, however, certain of my human's love, he simply turned from the food, raised his tail high in the air, tipped its end, and showed me his behind as he sauntered from the room.

Still, I sang my denunciation. While it did not affect Tybalt, my human would perhaps understand the depths of my loathing and the firmness of my resolve to remain in the pantry until he disappeared from our midst.

When summer came, I stayed outdoors, never coming inside except to eat. Since Tybalt's arrival, I had not entered the front rooms of the house or gone upstairs. I never willingly approached my human, and when she insisted on picking me up, I turned my face away and struggled from her arms.

At the approach of winter, I returned to the pantry. I had avoided my human for an entire year. While she lay on the couch in the front room and read, I plotted on my pantry shelf. While she slept upstairs, I roamed the back of the house and pondered dark thoughts. She had made a serious mistake in bringing this trouble-maker, this Tybalt, this tyrant into my home. I would not hurt him—that was not my way. But I would make my statement.

Each day, I yowled disgust to demonstrate my resolve to remain in the pantry until Tybalt disappeared.

Finally, my human came. Lifting me down from the shelf, she cuddled me close. As she smoothed my fur, she murmured, "I'm sorry, Dulcy. You're right. This is your home too. I didn't know that Tybalt would upset you so."

How could she not know?

Shortly after that, Tybalt left. When I heard the front door close behind him, I leaped to the pantry floor. For the first time in a year, I strolled into the living room where my human sat, sobbing. With majestic calm, I jumped onto her lap, stood upright, and tapped one front paw against her face. Well done, I told her. Well done!

She laughed through her tears. "A farmer took him, Dulcy. He'll like the farm. I know he will."

She smoothed my face and touched her cheek to mine. How good that felt after the bleak months I had known. How good she smelled. How much I loved and needed her.

$\mathcal{S}$ t a r t i n g
O v e r

Shortly after the accursed Tybalt left us, I noticed that Bartleby was sick. My human noticed too. Several times she took him to the vet. But as the months passed, he lost weight. His face became gaunt; his eyes bulged. He was only eight, but he was failing quickly.

One day in late winter, my human carried Bartleby from the house. She returned from the vet's with a heavy plastic bag. Tears trickled down her face.

I followed her behind the garage. There she carefully laid down the plastic bag and tested the ground until she found a soft spot. Then she dug a hole and placed the bag in it.

"Good-bye, Bartleby," she sobbed. "You were pure joy to me. I'll never forget you. Never. Thank you for coming to live with me. I'll always love you."

I knew then that a chapter of our lives had ended.

My human covered the plastic bag with dirt and filled in the hole. Sadness splintered the pattern of her life. She cried for many days. When I nudged her cheek, she folded me in her arms and dripped tears onto my fur. "Bartleby's gone, Dulcy. *Gone.* He'd better be in heaven because I don't want to go there if he's not."

I felt the loss of Bartleby too. The house was empty of the presence of one who knew how to love and how to accept love. I missed him. Sometimes I roamed the rooms looking for him. I visited all his special places. But I never found him. He was with the great god of cats.

For long days my human grieved. And I? I showed her all my love. I reached back into our past, into our first year together; I gave her my sweetness as never before.

When she lay on the couch, I leaped onto her chest, wove intricate circles, and settled against her. Since New Hampshire, the only time I had done this was when she was sad unto death.

Now, whenever my human ate her breakfast, I jumped up on the table and laid my chin against her forearm. She laid down her spoon and stroked my fur. A smile lit her face, and she murmured loving words to me. "It's just you and me now, Dulcy. At the end of all these years, it's just you and me."

With Bartleby gone, my human needed company at night. After she settled in bed, I placed a paw on either side of her neck and kneaded the pillow while resting my nose against her cheek. When she lightly held me to her beating heart, I purred love. My chest reverberated with the sound. Surprise gladdened her face. She had not heard that purr for many years. I sang her the ballad of our life together:

> *Be still, my human.*
> *Be gracious to yourself.*
>
> *I know your grief.*
> *I know you miss the joy*
> *of Bartleby.*
>
> *I miss him, too,*
> *my kit,*
> *my kin.*
>
> *He was gift from the god—*
> *to you,*
> *to me,*
> *to us together.*

Now I know—
true as the day's dawning
after the hunt—that
we,
we, too, are gift.

I need no more.
Our love, our life
is enough.
Yes,
more than enough.
This, too, is gift.

All is gift—
this present day,
yesterday, tomorrow.

We,
we two,
are one.
As we have always been.

Certain am I
of your love, my human.
Oh, then,
be certain, too.

Lulled by my song, my human murmured, "I know, Dulcy. We will always be together. Always." Purring my comfort, I gave my love wholly, and she gave hers.

Making My Dream
Come True

In the years following Bartleby's death, my human has learned my subtlest meow, my slightest purr. These eight years have been unforgettable for me and for her, too, I think.

The memories of these years are soft. I see them in the light of her love and care. I dream these memories as I snooze beneath the bushes by the house. My human centers her life around me. To her, I am human; to me, she is cat.

She understands my needs. When I want a massage, I come to where she is and gaze at her. She looks down and speaks softly. "Dulcy. What is it? Are your bones weary?"

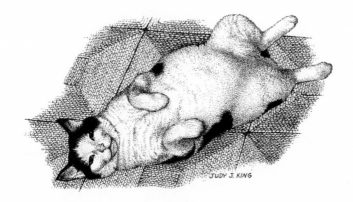

JUDY J. KING

Awaiting her touch, I lie on my back with my stomach upward and my paws lifted to air. She never fails me. My human settles next to me on the floor and rubs her palms back and forth over my stomach. Upward and downward her hands caress my fur. Then she turns me on one side and kneads my skin and legs and paws.

Next she rubs my other side. Finally, she places me on my back again and stretches my two front legs backward, slowly and deliberately. Because of this, I have never, even now when I am old, suffered from arthritis. With these massages, my human keeps my joints supple and my heart content.

To oblige me, my human stopped leaving each day and began to work at home once more. She bought a computer and spent long hours staring at green words on a black screen. I sat nearby and talked to her. Often she reached down to touch my fur and to tell me how wonderful I was.

Sometimes, when I lay on the floor with my belly up, my human gently rubbed her foot back and forth over my fur. Then I grabbed hold of her shoe and she shook me from side to side.

As the years passed I found myself increasingly dependent on her presence. Without my human in it, the house was no home. When she was away, even for a few hours, I felt lonely; when she returned, I showed my love by wreathing her legs and purring a song of these new days:

Only when you are home,
my human,
only when you are home
am I content.

With you away
my days are bleak, unkind.

I sleep; I yawn;
I guard our house
against the one
who comes too near.

With you at home
my days are soft, benign.
I dream; I sing;
I greet your purr
with lick of hand
and weave of dance.

Then memories I give to you.
Memories of the deep sweetness,
the dark sweetness,
the everlasting sweetness
that is my love.

Be home to me.
Oh, human, be ever home.

Working at her computer, my human often concentrated so hard that she forgot about me. An hour of inattention passed; she did not look at me; she did not stroke my fur or massage my stomach. I tolerated this neglect for only so long. Then I walked across the keyboard, leaving tiny squiggles on the screen behind me. She needed these gentle reminders that I was her first concern.

When I came to her and meowed my needs, she always stopped what she was doing and centered her attention on me. She held me in silence or talked to me or napped with me or enjoyed a snack with me. She put aside working at the computer. Often she exclaimed, "I love you, Dulcy. You are the sweetness in my life."

Like a cat, she learned to enjoy these moments, to cease her worry about finishing things. Unlike most humans, she learned to live in the present.

Studying Each Other's Needs

When my human accepted how I wanted to be held, she truly became an unwhiskered cat. I did not like to be carried against her chest, with my face peering over her shoulder. No, I wanted to be held in her folded arms with my stomach upward, my gaze resting on her face. That way I could see love shining from her eyes.

I liked to be close to her body. When she lay on the couch in the front room and read, I lithely stepped over or around the book and settled on her chest. "Dulcy! Hello," she'd greet me. "How are you? Do you want to rest awhile?"

She never removed me from her chest and placed me on the floor. No, she let me sleep while she daydreamed or lay still without the lure of printed words. Sometimes she, too, fell asleep. When we woke, she spoke to me softly, recounting the story of our life together. Afterward, I wandered off and left her to her book. She pleased me entirely.

My human brought home, just for me, a blue plaid blanket. She placed it on a chair in the living room. There I slept when she was away. And often when she read, I lay on my blanket and watched her with eyes dark with love. Just being in the same room was contentment to last a lifetime.

Sometimes she would look across the room at me and say, "Dulcy, you're going to live to be twenty or even more, aren't you? Will you promise me that? Will you?" Her tenderness engulfed me. But I could promise nothing. Only the present was my gift to her.

My human often carried me outside to the garden and told me the names of her favorite flowers. "This is astilbe, Dulcy. And this is phlox. Over here is bee balm. Don't get too close to it when you come outside. The bees will sting."

When we returned to the house, she put music on the stereo, held me against her shoulder, sang words of love, and danced around the kitchen.

I really didn't like this. However, I yowled no protest nor did I scratch her—I had never scratched my human. Instead, I stared into the far distance, longing to be doing anything but dancing! Finally the song would end and she would put me down.

"Wasn't that nice, Dulcy? Don't you like to dance? I love to dance." Because this pastime pleased her, I endured it.

What I did like to do was survey the world from a high place. However, because of my weight and advanced age, I wasn't good at climbing trees anymore, so my human helped me find a vantage point from which to gaze at my universe. When the urge for height took hold of me, I sat in the kitchen and looked longingly at the ceiling.

Then she set a chair in front of the lower cabinets, picked me up, stepped onto the countertop, and placed me on top of the cupboards. I roamed the flat surface of them and let my gaze follow my human as she worked. When I grew weary of the height, I drew her to me with silence. Obedient, she got up on the counter and lifted me down.

During these years I invented a new game. I would lie on the floor, and when my human walked by, I would try to capture her feet. She always laughed at my antics and then sat on the floor with me. She rubbed and scratched my stomach, her fingers lifting the fur, touching my skin.

In an ecstasy of love, I grabbed her hand between my paws, seized her index finger between my teeth, and thumped my back paws against her hand. I bit down to hold her close, but I never marred her skin. I loved her so much when this happened that I wanted to eat her. My eyes turned liquid with love. Truly she was mine. Sometimes I meowed "Where do you end and I begin?"

$\mathcal{C}$ a m p i n g
To g e t h e r

For many years after Bartleby's death, my human disappeared each September with one of her friends. Days before they left, she lugged camping equipment from the basement to the kitchen. As soon as the Coleman stove and lanterns appeared, I prepared myself for a time of desolation.

After loading the equipment into the car, my human and her friend would get up very early one morning and leave—always with soft words for me, always with assurances that she would miss me and that she would return, always with a final caress. But always they left me behind. The days stretched endlessly.

Oh, yes, someone came to feed me, but this was not *my* human. She did not smell of baby powder; she did not scratch under my chin; she did not hold me in the cradle of her arms.

When my human returned from these trips, I welcomed her with the deep rumble of my purr and the rasp of my tongue. Despite my loneliness, however, she continued to leave me home when she camped each year.

After years of this, I stopped eating and grooming myself during one of these camping trips. When my human returned, I looked decrepit. Together we sat in a chair and talked. I purred and meowed and told her of the loneliness of the days, the darkness of the nights, the pain of her desertion:

The days are dark
when you are gone.
Dark and ever dreary.

My heart is heavy
when you are gone.
Heavy with the mystery
of where you are
and when you will return
to be with me again.

Don't go!
Don't go!
Don't ever go away
again!

I beg you;
I beseech you;
I entreat you.
As you love me,
stay.

The next year, I became a camper. The three of us—my human, her friend, and me—traveled north to a distant park. After they set up the tent and prepared it for habitation, my human placed me within its narrow confines. Immediately, I stationed myself at the front.

When she returned with more paraphernalia and unzipped the entryway, I jumped through the open flap and ran toward the bushes. Darkness hid me from view. From my place in the underbrush, I could hear the panic in her voice. "Dulcy! Dulcy! You could get lost. Come back!"

Furtively I stepped over the leaf-strewn ground. But my human heard me and swooped. "I got you! Thank heavens, I found you." She quickly deposited me in the tent. This wasn't starting out to be any fun at all.

The night was cold, and I crawled inside my human's sleeping bag. (I felt the cold more than I used to.)

The next day, when I left the confines of the tent, my human ensnared my body with a harness and leash. I who had always found my way home even from my longest treks at night!

With an adroit twist of my body, I shrugged the harness aside. Then I trotted down the road and headed toward the underbrush, knowing she would follow me into the briars, cowed.

The next day the two of us walked around the loop on which our campsite was located. After that we walked two or three times a day—in the morning after she and I had breakfast; in the afternoon after she returned from being away from the camp; and in the evening before she sat down by the fire to read and play games.

Like a true unwhiskered feline, my human let me determine where we would walk and how long we would spend at each point of interest. Sometimes our walks lasted for over an hour.

Much of the loop where we camped was empty. As we came to each campsite, I left the road and wandered over the grass to investigate the smell of the fire ring and the greasy splotches on the tables.

I sniffed the evidence of canine brute, examined the hiding places beneath the surrounding bushes, and drank the rainwater that lay in pools around the site. (I seemed to be drinking a lot more water.)

My human stood on the road and laughed at the thoroughness of my detection. "You missed a spot, Dulcy. Be sure to sniff that twig!" Pleased with her, I returned to where she waited. We walked a few

JUDY J. KING

more steps and I left again to explore another campsite. I looked forward to our daily treks.

When we walked at night, she centered the ray of a flashlight on me. I moved quickly through the underbrush as I scented the animals lurking there. But when I went too far into the woods, she stumbled through the high grass and swept me into her arms.

One night while we camped, a sudden attack of thunder shattered my sleep. Terrified, I shot into the air, yowled, and fell with a thud onto my human's stomach.

"Dulcy! Dulcy!" She flayed her arms in the dark, searching for the lantern. "It's okay! It's okay!"

I scooted inside the sleeping bag to the haven of her body. Trembling, I complained about the accommodations as the menacing storm echoed across the lake.

Another night an eerie noise came from beyond the tent, and my human unzipped the flap to peer outside. Frenzied I leaped through the opening.

"Dulcy! Dulcy! It's too dark out. I can't see you. Where are you? You'll get lost!"

I ran past our picnic table and into the next campsite where a trailer stood. Just then a flash of lightning illuminated the dark, and my human, seeing the blur of my white fur, shouted, "Dulcy! Stay there."

Frightened, I dashed for safety beneath the trailer, but my human hurled herself through the air and grabbed my hind legs. Both of us flopped on the sodden ground, and I hissed my mortification.

She wiped my fur and crooned a song of relief to me. I spent much of the night grooming myself and then snuggled next to her warmth.

The lazy days continued until one morning my human and her friend put me in the car and dismantled the tent. Short hours later we were home again and I rushed to the pantry for water.

Water and warmth. I craved both.

$\mathscr{F}$alling Ill

When my human noticed that I was drinking more water, we visited the vet, who gave us pills. This happened in early October.

Because I was too weary to wander outside, my human put a mattress in the middle of the porch floor. During most of the cool fall days, I slept there. The sun warmed the mattress covering, and I dozed in a patch of brilliant light, dreaming of the chase.

By early November, I had no energy left to venture onto the porch. My appetite was gone, and I stopped eating.

We went to the vet again, and I stayed overnight. Imprisoned in that small cage, I missed my human. The listless cats surrounding me echoed my own condition.

She came the next day. I had no strength with which to greet her. She stood by my cage and talked to the vet about me. Exhausted, I could attend to only a few of their words. He said my kidneys were bad and my human should put me to sleep.

She cried. I forgot my lethargy and pressed my face against the cage. I longed to comfort her, but I had no energy to meow my concern.

"No. Not now. Not yet. In a day or two. I need time to say good-bye. When Bartleby was sick, you said put him down right now. And we did. But that was a mistake. I needed time to say good-bye."

Tears coursed down her cheeks. She kept shaking her head in denial. Then she peered into my cage and put a finger through the bars to smooth my forehead.

"No, not like Bartleby. I won't let that happen with Dulcy. I won't. I've learned something in these eight years. I need time to say good-bye. We've lived together so long. We have to have time to say good-bye."

The vet opened the cage. My human's gentle hands lifted my body, and she held me to the warmth of her chest.

"Oh, Dulcy," she cried. "What will I do without you? What will I do?" Her voice sounded frail and confused. I ached for her.

We left that accursed place of bad news and baneful deeds, and my human took me home. The house was the same, but I had changed.

My human and I sat on the couch. She buried her face against my side. Her tears speckled my lusterless fur, but I could only crouch in her lap, dulled by weariness.

"Dulcy," she sobbed, "you promised to live to be twenty. You promised! You promised me! You can't die now. You can't!"

I understood the words. But what I understood even more was the desperation of her voice. Would I leave her an orphan? What would she do without me? I had to try and live—for her.

My human often wept during this time. Sometimes she clutched me too close, but I allowed this. She begged me to get well, but daily I felt myself slipping away from her.

She stopped giving me the tuna that I loved and the soft kernels of food that tasted so good. Instead she fed me the canned food and the new nuggets that the vet had given her. Both tasted like sawdust.

I refused to eat these things.

"Dulcy, that other food has too much protein in it. Your kidneys can't deal with protein. You have to eat this special food. You have to. Please eat it."

But I didn't listen. The food was boring.

To arouse my appetite, my human often carried me to the pantry and stretched out on the floor next to me. Holding a spoonful of canned food beneath my mouth, she encouraged me to eat. To please her I sniffed at it and nibbled a small bit.

"Dulcy, thank you for trying so hard. I know that you don't like this food. But please eat it. Please."

She was so grateful for each bite. Still, the food tasted like mouse dung, and I could eat little.

Days passed; now I ate nothing. I grew weaker. My fur lost its luster. Even in my human's arms, I felt listless.

Finally one night she set a bowl of tuna before me and began to cry. But I hardly noticed her tears because the tuna tasted so good. I gobbled it while she rested her hand on my back.

"This is the end, Dulcy. You're too weak to go on, and I can't keep you just for me. You might as well have a last meal you enjoy."

She lay down on the floor by me and sobbed.

The next day she carried me to the chair by the phone, held me on her lap, and called the vet. She cried as she talked to him.

"It's time," she said. "I can't keep Dulcy alive any longer just to please myself. It's time to let go."

Then she told him about the tuna. Suddenly her expression changed. "Really? Really?" she said. "Oh, thank you. Thank you for telling me that."

Hanging up the phone, she gathered me to herself. I reached out one soft paw to touch her smile, and she babbled delight. "Dulcy! Eating the tuna showed that you still have an appetite. The vet said that's a good sign. I can give you the tuna water on your dry food and maybe you'll eat that."

She smoothed my fur and held me up so that we could look at one another. "Dulcy, isn't this wonderful! I don't have to let you go yet!" She smiled through her tears. "There's a treatment another vet will do! We'll be together longer. We will, Dulcy! We will!"

My human sang that day.

$\mathscr{F}$ i n d i n g   H e l p

The next morning we traveled to visit another vet. This time I did not yowl my annoyance from the rear window. I was too sick.

My human took me to a small room and placed me on a cold metal table. A man with a soft voice examined me. Then he placed a dish of warmed food in front of me. I wasn't interested. Next he stuck a needle in me. I gave a weak meow of protest and dropped onto the table. My face plopped into the food. I felt a surge of appetite and ate a few bites of the noxious stuff that my human had been feeding me at home.

Soon my human left; I was too lethargic to say good-bye. I stayed at this place all day; twice the vet put a needle in my skin and dripped a clear fluid into my body.

In late afternoon she returned for me. When we left, I crumpled against her, bone weary. She held me close. "Dulcy, I love you so much. I want you to live for as long as you can. For as long as you can enjoy life. The vet said you're not suffering."

My human sang a song to me as she smoothed my fur and rubbed my whiskers back against my cheeks.

"This new vet says I can give you the water treatment he did today. That will keep you from getting dehydrated."

As we drove toward home, I lay on her lap and she rested one soft hand on my fur. Her sweet voice played over me. "Dulcy, every day you live is a gift to me. But please help me to let go when the time comes. Help me to know when it's time, Dulcy. I never want to hurt you by holding on too long."

I treasured her words of love. Still, I felt so tired. Could I last through the night? What would my human do if I should leave her?

At home, I lay on my favorite chair—the brown corduroy one with my blue plaid blanket on it. I was hardly able to raise my head. I felt that I could hold on no longer, but my human knelt by my chair and smoothed my limp fur. She laid her soft lips against my forehead. Her gentleness surrounded me. She willed me to live through the night, and I knew that I must.

The next day my human pushed a large pill down my throat. She said that the pill would increase my appetite. But what it did was quite different! For the first time in my life, I had a bowel accident.

Feeling an overwhelming urge to go to the kitty litter, I dragged my weary body down the stairs and stepped into the litter box. My feces were wet and loose. I was so weak that I fell in it and matted my fur in its filth. Frightened, I stumbled upstairs to my human, mewing my dismay.

Cleaning me, she spoke ruefully. "Oh, Dulcy, how embarrassed you must be. You've always been so fastidious. I'm sorry, Dulcy. So sorry."

Hours later I fouled myself again.

My human gently cleaned me and whispered soothing words. "It's all right, Dulcy. It's not your fault. If this medicine makes you do this, we'll just stop taking it. I won't make you go through this mortification. I promise."

I heard her call the vet, but I was too tired to listen. The next day she gave me only a small sliver of the pill—once in the morning and once in the evening. I had never liked pills, and so I resisted these. But she insisted.

However, my appetite did increase, and I began to eat a little of the food she placed before me. She heated the food now, and it tasted better.

And so winter passed. Several times a day, my human tried to entice me to eat. She warmed the food in the microwave. Carrying me to the pantry, she lay on the rug and fed me with a spoon. I could not deny her. And so, even though I felt too weary to eat, I nibbled the offensive mush.

The pill my human gave me in the evening sometimes made me a little hungry during the night. When I felt the urge to eat, I woke my human and mewed my hunger. She always rose immediately and carried me downstairs where she heated my food. While I ate, she lay on the floor next to my bowl, stroked my fur, and talked to me in her sleep-filled voice about how much she loved me. I was able to swallow only a small amount, but even this pleased her.

As winter turned to spring, I ate more during the day. Thus, my human did not need to get up two or three times in the night to feed me. The two of us settled into a routine. She took care of me; I did all I could to respond.

Comforting Each Other

Once each week my human drip-ped a clear liquid into my body. One of her friends held me on the table. Then my human inserted a needle underneath my skin and the water from a bag dripped through plastic tubing and into my body.

This procedure didn't hurt me, so I scuffled for only a brief moment and then lay calm, content to do whatever my human wanted. Only once did she cause me any pain when inserting the needle. That time, I yowled and writhed in discomfort. But in the weeks that followed she never hurt me again. She was always gentle.

By the next day, I was better—less weary, more relaxed, at peace again. And so I did not mind these weekly needle sticks.

Despite the water treatment, I was still thirsty much of the time. I needed many watering holes. I had always liked variety, but now I wanted water within easy reach wherever I was.

When I was first sick, I could not leap onto the counter by the bathroom sink and drink as I had always done. So my human used three boxes to make a series of steps and kept the sink filled with fresh water. Thus, I could satisfy my thirst any time during the day or night.

As the weeks passed and my craving increased, my human put water containers throughout the house—in a yellow pie dish in the living room, a plastic margarine container upstairs, and a glass bowl in the pantry. Because I especially liked water that had drained through dirt, she put extra large containers under the houseplants and watered them often. Now I also did something I'd never done throughout our life together—I drank from the toilet.

I continued to eat the nuggets softened with tuna water and the other food that she heated. Still I lost weight. This brought agility. I climbed to the top of the Queen Anne chair in the living room and jumped onto the asparagus fern that stood behind it. The planter was, I discovered, a wholly satisfactory place to sleep. Some days I felt like a kitten again—sprightly and nimble.

At Christmas, friends of my human sent toys—a small stuffed stocking with a bell at one end and a stuffed carrot that had plastic suction cups at the ends of its feet and arms. My human dangled the stocking in front of me. To comfort her, I batted it. She dragged a ribbon in front of me; I pounced. She made the carrot dance; I swiped at its feet. This gave her such pleasure!

I noticed that as I lost weight so did my human. She and I had always had an agreement—if one of us lost weight the other would. Now we grew thin together. And I began to feel the cold as never before.

Because of this, and because I longed to comfort my human, I began sleeping with her. I even crawled under the covers. Before turning off the light each night, she read for long minutes. She sat with her head and back against the pillow propped against the headboard, with her knees up, and with her feet planted on the mattress. Then she pulled the blanket up to her neck and made a tent over her knees.

Jumping onto the bed, I crawled under the tent and rested my face on her warm feet. When she turned out the light and lay on her side, I woke and crawled into the curve of her chest where I rested my face on her soft hand. Together we slept through the dark winter nights, absorbing one another's body warmth.

I felt the cold during the day too. To help me, my human pulled one end of the comforter on the couch over the armrest to make a small tent under which I could sleep.

During that long winter, I spent each morning in the front window and scrutinized the neighborhood to see what changes night had brought. My human lay on the couch and prayed. When I had assessed the possibilities for the day, I padded across the back of the couch and jumped onto her chest. Then we prayed together to the great god of cats.

She watched me carefully and held me often. Again and again she recounted the story of how we had selected one another. She mused over our days in New Hampshire. She reminisced about Bartleby and our life together. She laughed about our year with Tybalt and apologized for her thoughtlessness. She thanked me for my love and for our life together. Always, she thanked me.

Each night my human lay on the couch and prayed again. I rested on her chest and listened to the words she said out loud: "Abraham, beseech the Lord for Dulcy. Sara, beseech the Lord for Dulcy. Issac, beseech the Lord for Dulcy."

She prayed through a litany of names: "Peter, beseech the Lord for Dulcy. Andrew, beseech the Lord for Dulcy. Matthew, beseech the Lord for Dulcy," she said.

The names rolled over me—Paul, Lucy, Cecilia, Benedict, Scholastica, Dominic, Francis of Assisi, Philip Neri, Peter Claver, Martin Luther King, Gandhi, Dorothy Day, Thomas Merton, Simone Weil.

Who were these people?

As she prayed, my head began to nod, my eyes to glaze. Succumbing to the beloved cadence of her voice, I fell asleep.

Depending on Each Other

Through the long winter of illness, I waited for spring. When it came, I began to go outside again. The rays of the sun warmed my fur and seeped into my skin. Now I spent all day and many nights outside, lying in my favorite places.

Often during the day my human opened the back door and came to find me. I could no longer hear her call, for I was deaf. Little by little during the winter my hearing had faded. I wish I had awakened one morning to the knowledge that that day would mark the end of hearing. How I would have treasured the moment that held my human's last soft words of love.

But I did not know. One moment I could hear faint sounds; the next, nothing. I would never again find comfort in the gentleness of her voice. Old age demands so much; we must let go so often; we must give up so completely. Denied my human's voice, I lived in a world of silence.

Now I did not hear her return home. Suddenly, I smelled her presence and felt her soft hand on my fur. Startled, I opened my eyes to discover her near. How could she be here and I not know? No longer was I doing my part—I failed to greet her when she returned. This saddened me. As I dreamed through long days, I found a new song, a psalm of age:

All sound is gone —
the growl of cur,
the scrape of key,
the creak of door,
the fall of her footsteps —
gone, all gone.

The song my human sings
I hear no more.
The whisper of her voice,
the sob, the purr, the laugh,
gone, all gone.

But the sound of love remains —
sweet memory,
wordless melody,
resting softly
within my heart.

And so when my human came outside on those warm days of spring and early summer, I did not hear her approach. But when my nose discovered her presence, I meowed my welcome. She knelt down by my hiding place beneath the bushes and smoothed my fur. How gentle her hand; how warm her fingers; how lovely her face.

Sometimes, she lifted me from beneath the bushes and talked to me. I could no longer hear her words, but I knew that love shaped them.

Holding me in her arms, she walked round the perennial garden. Her lips moved, and I knew from summers past that she was reciting the names of the flowers to me — astilbe, anthemis, coreopsis, daisy, bee balm, lily, baby's breath, malva, and my favorite, bleeding heart.

Then she carried me back to where she had discovered me and laid me, oh so gently, on the ground to rest. Again and again throughout the day she came to talk to me, to smooth my fur, to cradle my body, to smile at me, to assure me of her love. No longer were we two; we had become one.

Once, during the spring, I got caught outside at night during a sudden rain shower. Always before when my human came to the porch door and called me to come in from the rain, I bounded down the sidewalk and onto the porch. But now I could not hear her voice. So I lay beneath the bushes that gave me only partial shelter from the downpour.

Suddenly I saw her shoes. She had come for me! For a moment I was angry with her. She knew I hated the rain.

How could she leave me out here so long? I yowled my anger and rushed down the sidewalk. She came running after me and reached to open the porch screen. The two of us dripped onto the kitchen linoleum.

When I looked at her sodden clothes and hair, I forgot my anger and remembered only that she had come. Weaving my body around her legs I purred gratitude. Then she wiped the raindrops from my fur and carried me upstairs to bed. Together, we slept.

$\mathcal{T}$aking Our Last Journey Together

Because I had become more agile, I could hunt again. I could no longer hear tiny feet in the grass, but my nose never failed me—and I had a youthful reputation to maintain. During the early days of spring, I brought my human a mouse and a mole and left them by the porch door.

The night I caught a second mole I found myself suddenly hungry and so, while waiting for daylight to come and my human to rise, I took one nibble of him and then another. Soon little was left of the mole, and for the first time in many months, I felt replete.

In late May I went hunting one night and was gone for several hours. In the early hours of morning, I returned and discovered a light on in the kitchen. This had never happened before. I scratched the door, wondering if something were wrong with my human. She came and picked me up. She was crying and I saw her lips move in mute explanation. Suddenly I knew. She thought I had gone away to die. She thought she had lost me. How foolish of her. I would not leave my human. When the time came to die, I would be with her.

As the days passed into early summer, I began to throw up food or bile each day. I always went to the basement to do this so that my human would not have a hard time cleaning it up. If she heard me retching, she came immediately to comfort me. She stroked my back and held me close. Soon I came upstairs and went outside to lie in the sun. In the laziness of a warm day, I forgot being sick.

Once again, I grew weaker. I could no longer jump off the counter by the bathroom sink. I was not steady on my feet when I landed. So after I had gained the countertop and drank my fill, I meowed my need. Then my human came to hold me for a few moments and to place me safely on the floor.

Besides the stairs that my human made from boxes in the bathroom, she now made stairs for me by the kitchen windows. Until that summer, I was always able to leap up to and through the open window. I could no longer make this jump.

So my human placed an orange chair next to the window. On the floor at the side of the chair, she put a bag of newspapers. On top of this bag she put a sack with two books in it side by side. Now I leapt to the top of the books, to the top of the chair. Then I crouched down and eased through the open window to the porch.

Because I was weak, I could no longer groom myself well. Licking my fur to remove the dust of the outside took too much effort. I looked scruffy. Still, my human loved me. I knew this with a certainty that made each day sweet.

In late June my human pulled the suitcase from the closet. Together we journeyed to her brother's home in Independence, Missouri. Our trip was long and hot.

As the miles passed, I became weaker and weaker. At our first stop for gas, my human looked over the seat to where I lay on the floor. I gave a weak meow to tell her that I was not well. Immediately she got water for me. Then she held me and her lips formed the words I treasured: "I love you, Dulcy."

When we took to the freeway again, she stopped often so that she could carry me to a shady place where I could walk and explore. Following me, she let me wander far afield. Always I walked back to her so that she could carry me to the car. But the car was hot; the wind's howling kept me from sleep. The trip was hard.

Finally, we arrived. I spent most days in my human's bedroom, but sometimes I went to the porch. She had removed the screen from the bedroom window so that I could leave the room and go onto the screened-in enclosure beyond it. During the day, I slept in a clothes basket in my human's room. At night I curled myself into the corner of the porch.

Each morning she came to the porch and carried me into the backyard. There I nibbled grass and licked the dew. I investigated the crawl space beneath the porch and found places to hide, in case I needed them. She sat on the steps and waited for me to return.

Too weary to wander far, I settled next to her. After a while, she picked me up and carried me onto the porch, where I rested in my favorite place.

Sometimes she forgot and left the door open that led from the porch to the dining room. Then I wandered in and ate the food in the bowls of the cats who lived in this house. I hadn't tasted food like that since I'd become ill. The nuggets these cats ate, though hard, were different from the ones my human now used to entice me at home. In my better days I would have scorned even this food, but now it tasted as good as catnip.

My human didn't like my eating these hard kernels and scolded me each time she found me with my nose in one of the cats' bowls.

"Dulcy, your kidneys can't handle that kind of food. Eat from your own bowl. Please."

But I ignored her and waited for the open door.

As the days passed, my renewed interest in food waned. I grew weaker. I could not stomach even the tuna juice. My human gave me the pills each day, but they did not increase my appetite.

Now I drank little water. Twice while we were at her brother's house my human leaked fluid into my body, but this had no effect.

We had lived through a winter and a spring. But we would not live through the summer together. I was slipping away from life. My human realized this for she held me through much of the day. Often when I woke I found her gazing at me with deep sadness.

Finally, we left this place. My human raced home through the morning coolness. I could feel the speed of the car. She had placed a large sheet of cardboard between the back window and the front seat so that the rays of the summer sun would not touch me. The night before she had put the kitty litter in the freezer so it was cool. I slept on it all the way home. But I could no longer meow my thanks for the coolness of my resting place. The time had come.

Still I longed to investigate everything that was new in our lives, and when we stopped in rest areas, I walked slowly and deliberately over the grass and explored the bushes. When my human carried me back to the car, I settled against her chest, content.

We were going home; once more we would be alone together. I would see the perennial garden and the bushes by our house. She would visit me as I lay in the sun. Perhaps I would feel better at home; perhaps I would find the strength to go on.

We got home in the early afternoon. My human carried me from the car to the bushes by the house, and I spent the rest of the day in the sun. Often she came to run her gentle fingertips over my fur. I watched her mouth whisper words of love. When the sun set, she did not force me to come in.

That night I wandered away. Restless with weariness, I wanted to find a place to lie down where I could slip peacefully into eternity. There I would share stories about my human with the great god of cats. And so I wandered far afield that night and found a place to die. I could not keep my promise to my human and be with her when I died. She would not let me go.

But as I rested, my human's need called forth my love. After so many years how could I leave her alone? And so, when morning came, I struggled to pull myself upright. My legs wobbled; I walked slowly. The sun was already high overhead when I finally found my place beneath the ash tree and settled weakly on the grass to await my human when she opened the porch door.

Soon she came to the screen and saw me; she rushed across the lawn and reached to pick me up. Her arms were my haven. I had known no other in all my years. Yes; it was here that I wanted to die. She tried to feed me, but I could not eat. I drank some water, and then I sat at the screen door waiting for her to let me out. Always the outdoors beckoned, but always my human's love summoned me home.

$\mathcal{S}$ a y i n g   G o o d - b y e

All day I lie on the sidewalk soaking up sun. She comes often to smooth my fur. I watch her lips move and see love crease her face and fill her eyes. I know that if my nature compels me to go away tonight, I will surely die.

But when the sun sets, my human carries me inside.

I lie in my chair on the porch—the chair in which I had slept so often during our many summers in this house. But no matter how I rest my body, I find no comfort. She comes and picks me up and cradles me in her arms.

I am so tired that I cannot talk to her; I cannot meow; I cannot hear. And when she looks at me, begging me to get well, to go on, I cannot look into her face for I know I must let go. This is not easy for me. I cannot imagine leaving her and yet I must. My body no longer does what I want it to do.

I can no longer leap on her bed; I can no longer walk with strength in my legs. The pills she gives me do not help. Water has no taste. I cannot purr my love for her. I have said good-bye to all that she has been to me.

My human holds me. I am sure she talks to me. But I do not have even the energy to raise my face so I can look into her anxious eyes. I feel what she is feeling. I know that fear camps inside her heart.

She does not want to say good-bye. She does not want to let go of me. But I can give her no comfort. All my being is turned inward. I do not know if I will see the sun rise tomorrow.

When deep night comes, my human leaves me on the porch and closes the back door. She wants me to have the night. But I want to be close to her, and so I creep through the window and into the dining room. I can go no farther; I lie down beneath the table.

When she comes downstairs during the night, she sees me there. She lies on the floor next to me and rests her hand on my side. Gently she smooths my fur. Love for me softens her face and brings tears to her eyes. In the comfort of her tenderness, I fall asleep.

When I awake, my human is gone. She is upstairs sleeping, but I cannot go there. As the night passes, I am very weary. I have struggled for a long time to be faithful, to be here for her. But now I must let go.

It is morning and I struggle to get up. I hunker down within myself and sit hunched on the floor beneath the dining room table. Nothing is right. The time has come. I want to tell my human this. I want to say, "I *cannot* live to be twenty! I would like to. I would like to please you in this. But I cannot."

She comes down the stairs and sees me here and rushes to pick me up. On her face, I see that she, too, knows the truth: This is our last day together. I have said my good-bye. My good-bye has been my whole life. I have given her the gift of myself; she has given me the gift of her love. I am content.

A friend comes over, the same human who was here each week for the water treatment. My human picks me up and carries me to the car. We drive that long distance to the vet. Even now I am curious; even now I wonder about the houses we pass and the cats in them and if the people they live with are unwhiskered cats or only pet owners. I look out the window, and my human holds me up so that I rest against her shoulder.

Finally we come to the vet's. We go into the waiting room. I see a dog. I give one last meow. It is the best I can do now to show my human that I still cannot abide these brutes with twelve-inch teeth.

We go into a room, and she lays me on the metal table. The doctor comes and looks at me. I know it is the end, but I wonder if my human does. She begins to cry as she has all morning. The tears roll down her face, but I am so tired that I cannot rest against her shoulder and give her peace. I cannot hear the words of love I know she is saying.

My human stands as close to me as she can. She holds my face between her gentle fingers and gazes into my eyes. I look up into her sweet face. "What is happening? What is happening?"

In our long years together, I have asked this question so many times and always she has answered me. "We are going camping," she would say. "We are going to the vet. We are going home. We are moving to New Hampshire. We are moving to the North Hill. We are going for a walk. We are moving to our very own home, Dulcy. To our own home."

Always she answered my question, and as she looks into my eyes this time, I know that once again she is telling me what is happening—we are saying good-bye.

I watch my human's lips—soft lips from which have always flowed words of love. I recognize her chant: "Thank you. Thank you. Thank you, Dulcy," she cries. Her gentle hands tilt my face upward. As I feel the prick of the needle entering my leg, her love surrounds me. We are one, now and always. The great god of the cats has blessed us. Tenderness floods my being. Gazing on her dear face, I offer my final song—the gift of our life together:

> *I know you!*
> *I know you!*
> *You are my human.*
> *And I?*
> *I am your Dulcy.*

E P I L O G U E

Dulcy died on the morning of July 6, 1989. I wrapped her in her blue plaid blanket and buried her behind the garage in the daylily patch. She lies next to Bartleby. On that evening, as I stood at her grave, Dulcy's promise comforted me: "I shall not leave you orphaned."

And so, in the dark days that followed, I listened to the memories planted in my heart and remembered the good news of our life together: We were one—we had always been. Beyond the possibility of any doubt, Dulcy loves me with an unending love. This book is her final blessing to me, as it is my last gift to her.

Dulcy was seventeen years, four months, and one day old when she died.

—Dee Ready, Dulcy's human

JUDY J. KING